Falan Blake is a chef and single mom. After years of working in the restaurant industry Falan decided to retire her chef career and write full time. She is the author of several publications and lives in Arizona. Over the years Falan has utilized the law of attraction to manifest her own business success and decided to share her tips here for creating the life you want in her journal. This journal assists you in creating a step by step plan for developing your best self and live the life you want.

can connect with Falan on her website www.AskFalan.com and podcast Ask Falan by subscribing to both you will be eligible for Amazon gift card drawing and an autographed copy of all her ks.

Predictive Manifestation
By Falan N. Blake

Creating the life you deserve on your own terms.

The Predictive Manifestation Journal by Falan N. Blake

Author Preface:

In the few chapters of this book I mention a brief synopsis of how I have come to manifest the reality I am currently living in. Absolutely everything we receive is a result of thoughts. In this book I will discuss with you how I have achieved some incredible outcomes as a result of believing in the law of attraction and following the Abraham Hicks formulas. This book is designed to make you feel uncomfortable in facing your inner subconscious mind in which holds you back from materializing your dreams, by making you face things you have suppressed. I am confident that this journal will lead you on the right path and offer you the best outcome in reshaping your mindset. Keep in mind this is a journal. It is up to you to write in the blank pages and track your progress. If you desire personal coaching. You are welcomed to take my E-Course from Vivid Vortex Academy.

The Predictive Manifestation Journal by Falan N. Blake

Dedicated to my family:

Mom: You died before I manifested the life I promised you. I will still achieve it in your memory. I miss and love you.

Dads: God sent you both to me when my mom passed. Thank you for stepping into the greatest parental roles a " daughter" could ask for. Your belief in me is why I wrote this book. I love you both.

Timani: You are the greatest daughter of all time. My existence today is so that I could be your mother. May this book allow you to have a more pleasant outlook on your teenaged life and learn how to manifest your desires a lot sooner than the 35 years it took me to fully implement. I love you infinitely.

Nick: Your very presence has captivated me from the first correspondence. You are indeed a light that has lit my path to achieving my highest self. I am eternally grateful for our unique and transcendent connection. We fell in love for a reason and I am so amazed that we did. You are exactly what I prayed for and there hasn't been a more perfect partner than you. May you find the secrets to manifest your best reality within these pages. I love you endlessly.

The Predictive Manifestation Journal by Falan N. Blake

Alexis: Mom would be proud of you. You just keep fighting! You will conquer your mind I am so certain of this. Never give up, I love you sissy.

Aunt Marcella: You are a blessing to have as a secondary mom. You have been the best role model of a successful woman in our family. I do what I do because of you. I love you to the moon! Keep striving for the best.

CONTENTS:

- ❖ Chapter 1.) The Power behind thought.
- ❖ Chapter 2.) The Subconscious mind.
- ❖ Chapter 3.) The 55x5 Manifestation Method
- ❖ Chapter 4.) Cognitive Reframing

The Predictive Manifestation Journal by Falan N. Blake

Chapter 1.

The Power of thought

Quotes: Change your thoughts and you can change your world. ~ Norman Vincent Peele.

Thoughts become things. ~ The Secret by Rhonda Byrne

I remember my mentor suggested **The Secret** in 2009. This year was the collapse of my first marriage. I was 23 years old and ready to leave my 6.5 year marriage. I hadn't been happy since the birth of our child upon discovering glimpses of infidelity in the search history of our family computer. It was only a matter of time before I'd plan my departure. With my constant negative state of mind, I created all the fears I had harbored in my subconscious and allowed them to manifest themselves into my reality.

Thoughts running through our subconscious minds can help us manifest the life we really want or project deepest fears. Whatever we think about consistently , we ultimately move toward the outcome or somehow will it to us like a boomerang. We really are the product of our own thought pattern.

The Predictive Manifestation Journal by Falan N. Blake

Some of you reading this will try to remain in the victim mindset of playing the blame game until you are ready to receive the message this book offers you.

I am living proof that we can create our own realities from intended thoughts. By dwelling on past hurts we create a stagnant energy and repeat past traumatic cycles of exactly what we don't want. This happens because we are energy, our thoughts are energy and the power of energy is the ultimate experience for manifestation. Negative thoughts can become parasitic to the mind and physically manifest itself into our reality.

In this chapter you will find a myriad of exercises one can do daily to gain control over your mind. There is power in writing out your intentions so this book is designed to allow you to write out and see your thoughts in a workbook form.

When one believes in themselves the possibilities are truly endless. We must search within the depths of our souls to find a way to accept ourselves as we are and know that it is ok to be flawed and yes, it is ok to fail at things but we must not live in the failed state of mind too long. Allow yourself to grieve momentarily, really feel the emotion and get through it. After this process is done, release it. Let go of that feeling and find what you learned from it and focus on what that taught you and how you can prepare your future self from repeating the cycle.

Positive Affirming

I AM BEAUTIFUL

Look at yourself in the mirror. Really look at yourself. Stand there naked and bare your soul out loud. Take in how you look and then visualize yourself the way you feel internally if you aren't already happy with the reflection staring back at you.

Most of us see physical flaws as a hinderance for our own characters. We tend to hide imperfections instead of embracing the uniqueness of our bodies. Remember you can change your appearance. Often time what we feel on the inside mirrors the outside and in some cases people who appear outwardly perfect are incredibly broken internally.

When you looked in the mirror how did it make you feel?

I felt _____

The Predictive Manifestation Journal by Falan N. Blake

Why?

_____

_____

What do you plan to do next to change what you see?

_____

_____

Name 3 physical characteristics that are your best features.

1. _____
2. _____
3. _____

Go back to the first memory of when you realized you felt unhappy with your physical appearance and if you are happy with your physical appearance go back to the first memory of when you felt like you were not at your physical best.

If you have any negative feelings about any of these things. I want you to close your eyes and feel the feelings of how you felt that day and pinpoint what emotions those were. When you can identify adequately the exact emotions you can prevent a triggered reaction from occurring again without your consent.

The Predictive Manifestation Journal by Falan N. Blake

What did you see when you closed your eyes and what did you feel emotionally?

_____
_____
_____
_____
_____
_____
_____
_____
_____
_____
_____
_____
_____
_____

Repeat this exercise every day for a week. See if you change your answers to the same questions daily. If you have not changed how you see yourself in 7 days . Repeat until you do see improvement in your responses. Remember everyone who reads this journal will be at different places in their life and it can take longer or less time to positively re-affirm your emotions about your appearance.

The Predictive Manifestation Journal by Falan N. Blake

Day 1:

In each box write what you feel today when you woke up.

The Predictive Manifestation Journal by Falan N. Blake

Day 2

Are you more aware of your physical appearance? What does today mean to you?

Explain:

Day 3

Ask a trusted friend to tell you the truth. Even if its harsh. Sometimes we are in denial and sometimes a trusted person will be your accountability partner. Whatever they said write below how it made you feel. Did you resonate with them? Sometimes we aren't ready to receive information. I can't express this enough to make sure this is a trusted person. If you don't have one. Do this exercise based off your physical appearance when it was at its best.

Explain:

The Predictive Manifestation Journal by Falan N. Blake

Day 4

What habits have you changed these past few days?

Explain:

The Predictive Manifestation Journal by Falan N. Blake

Day 5

Are you ready for this journey this time? Say Goodbye to the old you. Your best self is at the finish line.

Tell me your 30 day goal?

Explain:

Day 6

As we come to an end of the first weekly exercise I want you to write in the space below something about you that you are most grateful for physically. Write it out in a single sentence until you reach the end if the page.

Example: I am grateful for my hands as they are the very source of my career's success.

What are you grateful for?

Day 7

Do you look any different from Day one? You should. Once the mind shifts, the body responds. You could be glowing, happier and appearing to be more energetic and focused. Now that you are aware you will naturally altar your appearance.

What has this exercise meant to you?

Explain:

Journaling space:

Add your before & after photo here. Switch it out as often as your appearance changes from doing the inner soul work. This is not about physical exercise. You will organically change physically.

Chapter Two

The Subconscious Mind

It's important to understand that the subconscious mind is a memory bank. Think of it as a piggy bank as a child you stored change in mindlessly until it filled up. Not every time you put in a coin you remembered. Your subconscious mind actually remembers ever dime you literally put in there, how you got the money and what you were wearing, the date, the time possibly and the weather. This is the power of the subconscious. It literally stores permanently everything that has ever happened to you. Your subconscious memories are perfectly intact. It's the conscious mind that gets clouded. This is why hypnosis can retrieve memories and traumatic experiences we repress that deliberately interferes with exactly what we want in our conscious mind.

When the subconscious and conscious are in conflict we tend to have that experience where we just can't seem to catch a break . (ex: Why can't we get that promotion, why doesn't so and so love me the way I love them, why can't I lose weight, why can't I get out this rut etc.) This is why reprogramming with self love and affirmations is paramount. Positive affirmations are very effective to change your thought patterns so that your conscious mind is in unison with the subconscious. This takes constant conditioning until you can do it naturally without the forced efforts. Understand that the subconscious mind cannot think independently. It will absorb the commands of the conscious mind and implement whatever you tell it. That is why it is so important to practice positive thinking so that your outlook on life is changed for the better.

It is our subconscious mind that keeps us breathing without us telling ourselves to breathe. Can you imagine having to remind yourself to breathe every second of the day? You couldn't do anything else and you could never sleep. EVER. So if you fell asleep and didn't remind yourself to keep breathing you would just die.

Our subconscious mind remembers all of our habits and quirks and will keep us in our comfort zones. The laziness of not wanting to fold laundry after its done is one of my quirks. After I completed the very tasks in this book I now do laundry from start to finish with a smile. I look forward to seeing the crisp folded clothes of laundry for the week. Before, I'd leave them in the dryer and wear them from there. Additionally, I'd never make up my bed because I am just going to get back in it, now I make it up even if I am going to the bathroom in the middle of the night. I retrained my subconscious to crave that freshness in bedding before laying in it. Your subconscious mind will make you feel uncomfortable when you start to do anything new to enhance your life for the best if you have lacked in that area. The subconscious doesn't like the new habit for doing laundry from start to finish or making your bed after you get up every single time. It is a pattern of behavior that keeps us in our comfort zone. This is why habits are so hard to break.

Try doing something different. Take a different route home from work and notice how uncomfortable you feel because you don't know what is coming around the corner.

Reprogramming your subconscious is an effort and task that isn't for the faint of heart. It will take much more proactive measures then what is sited in this journal. My journal is designed to just give you a guideline to help you become aware of these nuances. My Academy is designed to keep you accountable period and help you help others.

Complacencies are the very enemy of the conscious mind because they will want to keep us in our comfort zones. If you are ready to commit to reconditioning your subconscious mind lets get into these exercises.

List the habits that need reprogramming.

1.)

2.)

3.)

4.)

5.)

6.)

The Predictive Manifestation Journal by Falan N. Blake

7.)

8.)

9.)

10.)

Habits are hard to break. Stress and complacency forms habits and these tools will offer an option to help you counteract that. One of my biggest habits is procrastination. This is the only habit I have that I have to keep on track of today.

- Surround yourself with people you admire to be just like
- Visually see yourself succeeding
- Choose to substitute the bad habit with a good habit because you don't remove it you just replace it. It's always there, but it is a choice.
- Cut out every trigger you can
- Be mindful of the words you use. No more negative self talk. Try to avoid saying BUT
Unless you add a positive spin to it. "*I am always late but I am working to arrive on time going forward.*"

It is ok to slip up, it happens but don't get complacent. Understand the first step is awareness. Take note of the mood you are in, where you are and any triggers to stop the bad habit. I cannot stress to you enough to live in the moment. REALLY live in it. We do so many mindless things that we lose time and wonder where the time went. When you are aware of timelines and time sensitive information you can really get the most out of your subconscious self to program it to do what the conscious mind wants to do, and that is to be your best self.

The objective here is not to judge yourself but to be aware. These small changes can really lead to some remarkable results.

Journal Space

Explain your processes in habit breaking for each habit:

The Predictive Manifestation Journal by Falan N. Blake

Day 1:

List one BIG habit to break and journal how you replaced it for 21 days straight. It's is said it takes 21 days to form a new habit. Let's get it.

Habit ONE: THE BIG ONE

GO:

The Predictive Manifestation Journal by Falan N. Blake

Day 2 :

The Predictive Manifestation Journal by Falan N. Blake

Day 3

The Predictive Manifestation Journal by Falan N. Blake

Day 4:

The Predictive Manifestation Journal by Falan N. Blake

Day 5:

The Predictive Manifestation Journal by Falan N. Blake

Day 6:

The Predictive Manifestation Journal by Falan N. Blake

Day 7:

The Predictive Manifestation Journal by Falan N. Blake

Day 8:

The Predictive Manifestation Journal by Falan N. Blake

Day 9:

The Predictive Manifestation Journal by Falan N. Blake

Day 10:

The Predictive Manifestation Journal by Falan N. Blake

Day 11:

The Predictive Manifestation Journal by Falan N. Blake

Day 12:

The Predictive Manifestation Journal by Falan N. Blake

Day 13:

The Predictive Manifestation Journal by Falan N. Blake

Day 14:

The Predictive Manifestation Journal by Falan N. Blake

Day 15:

The Predictive Manifestation Journal by Falan N. Blake

Day 16:

The Predictive Manifestation Journal by Falan N. Blake

Day 17:

The Predictive Manifestation Journal by Falan N. Blake

Day 18:

The Predictive Manifestation Journal by Falan N. Blake

Day 19:

The Predictive Manifestation Journal by Falan N. Blake

Day 20:

The Predictive Manifestation Journal by Falan N. Blake

Day 21:

Fun fact:

The 21 day rule originated from a book in the 1970s called "Pyscho-Cybernetics . It was a self help book much like this one.

There is no such psychological proven concept as the 21 day rule but it's a nice goal to set for yourself so that you attain the new habit anyway.

You did it! How do you feel?

Explain:

CHAPTER 3

THE 55 x 5 METHOD

This method has completely and utterly changed my entire life. I am so excited about this chapter because you are about to really see how this method manifests your deepest desires. You were not ready for this method until you did the AWARENESS AND SUBCONSCIOUS exercises. Now that you have implemented new strategies for success you can literally manifest just about anything.

Fun FACT: You can manifest $1 million dollars just as easily as manifesting $1. Its all in the belief. Keep in mind that manifesting can take time but a million dollar idea can manifest immediately. It is all about the technique. This book, although not a typical book, is my million dollar idea. It embarks on the journey to creating the life I want which is to run a multi-million dollar home based business that teaches others to do the same. I want to work from home because commuting is not fun. If I want to get into work mode the farthest I want to walk is the next level of my home. I additionally want to travel the world. So in creating this life I use the 55 x 5 Method. Google it! It's a thang honey!

The Predictive Manifestation Journal by Falan N. Blake

What is the 55 x 5 Method?

It's a technique that accelerates manifestation. Whatever goal you set, you literally write it down 55 times for 5 days straight. This is the complete basis of this journal. All the other chapters are filler. It was necessary filler to help you understand how this works and to get you in the habit of using this to change your mindset. I tried telling my friends and family but they were not ready to receive it. If you made it this far into my journal, then you are ready for this lifestyle. I am literally writing this chapter at 4 am eating a peanut butter and jelly sandwich. This is THE LIFE. ☺ I can do what I want when I want. I am only working to gain skills I otherwise would have to pay to get in school. I literally can work a job that will teach me and pay me to do it and I can walk away from it and apply it to my OWN business and work from home. This is exactly the best way to reframe your mindset. I will tell you how to do that in the following chapter and in my virtual coaching academy.

The 55 x 5 method is combined joint effort of Manifestation, Predictive journaling and the Law of Attraction.

I will be brutally honest. This technique may not be for you. It is time consuming, your dream may be too long to write out and you may get tired or to busy to do it for the 20-30 minutes for 5 days. THIS IS OK TOO.

Why it works though is it's reprogramming your subconscious mind. Remember in Chapter 2 how I explain the subconscious works on its own from a level of comfort. It doesn't know right from wrong, it just is a infinite memory bank of all the things you have every done in your life. Essentially, Pandora's box!

This technique is supposed to be uncomfortable to do. It's a habit you want to break. You can't type this out you literally have to write to out. By writing it out you trick the subconscious to think it already happened so your conscious mind will allow you to do things that will bring you in alignment with whatever it was you wrote.

The 55 x 5 method is not a magic spell its more of a forced implanted memory. I don't know if you ever watched Spy shows like Alias with Jennifer Garner. She had her mind reprogrammed by having endless situations played for her on movies while being held captive. She literally had a whole chunk of her life missing because she had an alternate identity in France. She was away from her lover Vaughn and he searched for her but she was not a prisoner she just thought she was someone else for a longtime to complete a mission set for her that only a Sydney Bristow could accomplish.

Okay my Alias reference is because I am a fan but it is utterly the best scenario I can give you.

I literally told my ex I will be his wife someday, the day we broke up. Every single action I take now is training my subconscious to believe I am already his wife.

Everything that I use for the 55 x 5 method is in alignment to bring us back together for marriage. If it isn't him, a better version of him will come.

So lets dive into this.

In the pages following write your heart out!

The Predictive Manifestation Journal by Falan N. Blake

Day 1 55 x 5

The Predictive Manifestation Journal by Falan N. Blake

The Predictive Manifestation Journal by Falan N. Blake

The Predictive Manifestation Journal by Falan N. Blake

Day 2 55 x 5

The Predictive Manifestation Journal by Falan N. Blake

The Predictive Manifestation Journal by Falan N. Blake

The Predictive Manifestation Journal by Falan N. Blake

Day 3 55 x 5

The Predictive Manifestation Journal by Falan N. Blake

The Predictive Manifestation Journal by Falan N. Blake

Day 4 55x 5

The Predictive Manifestation Journal by Falan N. Blake

The Predictive Manifestation Journal by Falan N. Blake

Day 5 55x 5

The Predictive Manifestation Journal by Falan N. Blake

The Predictive Manifestation Journal by Falan N. Blake

The Predictive Manifestation Journal by Falan N. Blake

Now that you have done your first 55 x 5 method you just need to let it go. It is now in your subconscious mind. When it manifest please come back to this page and sign it with the date and time. Make note of the dates because you will want to know how long it took to manifest.

This next chapter is dedicated to what the academy teaches so I will keep it brief.

Chapter 4

Cognitive Reframing

What is Cognitive Reframing?

It's is a psychological technique that takes negative thoughts, memories, and emotions by reframing them in a more positive way. Example: I am not good at math. I utterly suck, I don't know how I don't get ripped off on my paychecks. I would never know.

Cognitive Reframing: I am not YET good at math, so I am identifying areas of struggle and finding a solution to understand those concepts so that I can better understand the breakdowns of my pay structure at work.

This process is actually used in Therapy. It is so vital to use it because it forces you to implement a new way of thinking for the subconscious mind. Remember it is a implanted positive seed all you need to do is plant it.

This is why I named my company Vivid Vortex with the tagline seeing things from a different perspective. Little did I know when I created this back In 2018 for the AskFalan podcast that I was planting the seed for this book and the virtual academy. I only created it for the podcast but because I practice what I preach, look where I am today? I birthed my million dollar home based business and now its coming into fruition.

The idea behind reframing your mindset is recreating the way you view a person, situation or circumstance. When you shift your mindset of the way you view that particular thing , often times your behavior will change with it. This is a good thing. This is what you want. What we need to realize is that there is always more than one way to look at a situation. It may not be ideal to look at everything from a positive perspective but it really changes circumstances faster when you do.

An example of reframing is when I wrote a check for the rent and it bounced even though I had the money in there, somehow the bank decided on not processing it because I had so many things coming out on ACH at one time that they rejected the most important thing.

 I panicked because I had to pay a late fee and subsequently I cried and said I just need to downgrade this giant palace for a smaller version for 6 months so I can breathe. I have a lot of travel coming up with speaking engagements, some paid and some not so I have to find a way to really simplify my lifestyle until I have more experience in doing what I do now. Instead of looking at losing my big home that I worked so hard for the last 18 months I am excited to save an extra $500 a month. I can really breathe with that modified added income. Oddly enough, as soon as I reframed the negative situation I attracted two extra income sources that tripled the savings amount.

I did think about staying put because now I have more income but to be honest I don't love the location of this place and its too noisy to film my podcast so moving really is the best bet for now until I move into the townhome I want.

This example is finding that silver lining. I encourage you to try this method on a situation.

There are two terms for this method: Cognitive Reframing which is what we do on our own and then Cognitive Restructuring is when we get the assistance from a therapist to help guide us to reframe by suggestion.

A lot of times we use emotional reasoning as a response to a situation by responding on how the occurrence affects us . How we feel is not necessarily accurate when we don't have all the supporting evidence. This internal feeling causes us to personalize the situation when it may not have anything to do with us directly but we take offense to it and in turn decide to reframe in a negative way. This is how a lot of miscommunication happens via text message.

I go into very detailed steps in my virtual academy on how to reframe and I talk about this on my TIK TOK : SheMotivates and Podcast :AskFalan so be sure to add me on both.

In closing of this chapter I want to leave you with a few tips on reframing/restructuring.

1. Calm yourself down in the situation first. BREATHE
2. Write down what triggered you.
3. Identify the feelings you have.
4. Write down everything you thought about when your mood shifted negatively.
5. Lastly, find the EVIDENCE to support and justify the situation.

It is likely we overreact when not needed too. I truly hope this mini journal inspired you to help you manifest the life you deserve. I am always here for you.

~Namaste

www.AskFalan.com

The Predictive Manifestation Journal by Falan N. Blake

What has this journal taught you?

Explain:

What is the most significant take away from the journal exercises?

Explain:

What is the next steps for you?

Explain:

The Predictive Manifestation Journal by Falan N. Blake

As a final thank you for being apart of a dynamic start of a journey I have planted years ago, I'd like to offer you 20% off on my next book The 48 HR Entrepreneur. This book discusses how to launch your business quickly and give you the steps needed to help you succeed from the start by avoiding the pitfalls I faced time and time again. Additionally, I am offering 55% off the Vivid Vortex Academy e-course for all who purchased/ received <u>The Predictive Manifestation Journal and followed me on all my social media platforms during the first quarter of the new year.</u>

Code: Namaste2020 for 20% off The 48 HR Entrepreneur

Code: Vortex2020 for 55% off the Academy.

The e-courses are designed for 21 days of restructuring. Spaces are limited because I am 100% invested in being active in the process.

Follow me on Instagram: @Ask.Falan

The Predictive Manifestation Journal by Falan N. Blake

Ms. Falan Nychole Blake

The Predictive Manifestation Journal by Falan N. Blake

Copyright : Vivid Vortex Resourcing & Media LLC 2020

www.ingramcontent.com/pod-product-compliance
Lightning Source LLC
Chambersburg PA
CBHW021023090426
42738CB00007B/878